Paranormal
Ghosts
of the University of Pittsburgh

Cover photo by Jennifer Yank,
Wikimedia Commons

Compiled by M. L. Swayne
Copyright 2010

Table of Contents

Introduction

Chapter 1: Pittsburgh Spirits

Chapter 2: The Cathedral of Haunting

Chapter 3: Alumni Hall

Chapter 4: Bruce Hall, Haunted Hall

Chapter 5: The Ghost of Lillian Russell

Chapter 6: Other Higher Ed Haunts

Chapter 7: Branch Campus spooks

Chapter 8: Bradford

Chapter 9: Johnstown, the City that Beat Death

Chapter 10: Greensburg's Paranormal Campus

Chapter 11: Titusville Area Terrors

Afterword: Why is Pitt haunted?

Tips: How to avoid haunted dorms

Introduction

At one time, Pittsburgh stood right at the edge of a haunted land, teetering between the known and the unknown.

In the mid- to late-1700s, Pittsburgh was a frontier town. To the west—beyond Pittsburgh's jagged borders—stood vast, unexplored regions. The dark Appalachian Mountains, once a seemingly impassable wall, silently watched over the small town, only to whisper stories of mystery and death, of settlers being swallowed up by its forbidden valleys, never to be seen again.

Just like the Allegheny and Monongahela rivers merge into the Ohio River in Pittsburgh, both fear and curiosity merge into an unquenchable desire for the people of Pittsburgh to move beyond borders, to explore the unknown.

This desire has turned the once small, insignificant frontier town into a pioneer of a different sort. It's a home base for science and industry. People like George Westinghouse and Andrew Carnegie lived there and made their fortunes. Some say that the pioneering spirits of Carnegie and Westinghouse, Frick and Mellon have never left.

Others—paranormal investigators and ghost hunters—say that the actual spirits of Carnegie, Westinghouse, Frick, Mellon and dozens of other famous Pittsburghers have never left their beloved city. They still walk the streets, float down the hallways, and peer out the windows of the city's famous buildings.

These investigators say that Pittsburgh's long past makes it ideal for hauntings. They also say the town has a boisterous, nervous energy—and if you were ever at Heinz Field during a rowdy Steeler game, you know what these ghost hunters are talking about. This energy connects the living with the dead, like the bridges cross and re-cross the three rivers.

These investigators into the unknown have collected plenty of proof of the "burghs" high rank in paranormal places. Haunted libraries, spooky abandoned factories, ghostly mansions, and spirit-filled public buildings and offices are just some of the sites that have been researched and classified as "haunted."

There are other places that are labeled haunted: the colleges and universities that make up the city's academic legacy. Universities, especially the city's namesake school, the University of Pittsburgh (affectionately tagged, "Pitt"), are generally the epicenter for stories of poltergeists, ghostly visits, and other urban legends.

The proud, old buildings of Pitt and other institutions and the fertile imaginations of its students, are fertile ground for stories about hauntings naturally abound. In the following pages, we'll take a ghost tour of the University of Pittsburgh, where modern skyscrapers are not immune to the presence of ghosts and where a banquet hall employs some unruly help, like a napkin-tossing poltergeist.

Pitt's academic aspirations reach to the skies, goals represented architecturally by the skyscraper-esque Cathedral of Learning, a building that some say, despite its modern look, is haunted by the past.

Other ghosts haunt the halls of Pitt, including one of Edgar Allan Poe's relatives and former hotel guests who never checked out.

The stories of University ghosts and poltergeists don't end at the campus borders; Pitt's branch campuses, which are located throughout the state, have ghost tales of their own. And most Pitt campuses, for some reason, find themselves in seriously haunted neighborhoods.

Since the University rests at the center of the haunted city of Pittsburgh, we'll explore some of the tales told about ghosts in the city. We'll also check out some haunted tales from other colleges and universities in the Pittsburgh area.

Chapter 1

Pittsburgh Spirits

Does the extra "h" stand for haunted?

The territory that would one day give rise to the city of Pittsburgh had always been a land of contrasts.

> Rugged and fluid.

> Barren and lush.

> Peaceful and full of conflict.

Pittsburgh is also a place where stories of the living mix easily with memories of the past.

It's in this contrast and in this conflict that Pittsburgh's haunted history was forged— a history of haunting that goes back centuries to the first days of the city's founding.

Pittsburgh's strategic value as a center for transportation and trade set competing cultures—native American and, later,

European—against each other for control of the region. Bloody battles and wars resulted. Some say those spirits still walk the ridges and valleys that make-up the city's haunted topography.

When French and English traders explored the region, another form of invasion started that would wreak havoc on the native cultures that had lived in western Pennsylvania for thousands of years.

Diseases—small pox, measles, and influenza—that Europeans had built a resistance to, devastated the native populations, who were defenseless against the microscopic invaders.

These stories, too, began to embed themselves into Pittsburgh's folklore.

Even today, stories filter back about ghosts of Native Americans who refuse to give up their land to strangers—even after death.

Reports of cursed properties are common. Contractors who build on areas that are under the auspices of these native powers report delays and accidents—some of them deadly. Builders say it is almost as though someone is trying to keep them away or is using these magical powers to continue their struggle to keep strangers and invaders out of their territory.

The spirits of Native Americans aren't the only ghosts who roam the Three Rivers area. As new cultures were introduced into the area, so were new ghost stories.

When Europeans colonized more and more of the frontier that became western Pennsylvania, territorial wars broke out between the native tribes and the vanguard of European explorers and pioneers. Pittsburgh became a killing zone.

Fort Pitt, located across town from the University of Pittsburgh, was one of those centers of death and violence. Located in what is now Point State Park, Fort Pitt is currently a museum. But during the French and Indian

War it was the scene of one of the conflict's bloody battles.

The battles haven't ended for some of these soldiers. Stories have been passed down about museum curators battling spiritual shoplifters. Objects disappear. And then reappear. Other stories about the haunted fort tell of strange voices emanating from quiet corners of the museum. When museum officials and visitors go to investigate, there's no one there.

The French and Indian War, and other inter-tribal violence, casts its supernatural shadow on activity in Pittsburgh; but, it wasn't the end of the violence, or the ghost stories.

Industries defined Pittsburgh. Its iron and steel mills, roaring with fires and molten metals, gave rise to the city's description as "hell with its lid off."

Not all that hell was under the giant vats of liquefied steel.

Labor unrest and other forms of violence are etched in the city's history, too. And, naturally, it is etched into the fiber of the area's supernatural lore. Natural disasters and industrial accidents, likewise, made Pittsburgh a perilous place to live and work.

Tales of factory ghosts are threads of Pittsburgh folklore that are woven into the city's hard-working, hard-haunting reputation.

One is re-told by S.E. Schossler in her book, *Spooky Pennsylvania*.

According to the story, workers at one Pittsburgh steel plant would watch as large buckets of molten steel, held by relatively thin chains, would glide over their heads. Each time one of the vats of hot metal would cross perilously overhead, it would remind the workers of some victim, who despite the highest attention to care and caution, would lose their lives in an accidental fall or a faulty piece of machinery. It was a quick—but gruesome—death.

There was one worker in particular—and the story of his brutal, accidental death—that haunted the employees of the plant, in more ways than one.

The worker accidentally tripped over a hose and landed in a kettle of molten metal. He was eviscerated. There were no remains for the family to collect, just a nugget of steel that was taken from the contents of the contaminated metal before it was tossed in a vacant lot.

The sudden loss of a favorite co-worker and the family's lack of closure hung over the mill workers in the days following the accident. It wasn't long before rumors started to be passed around that the worker, who seemed to vanish off the face of the earth, did not completely exit the premises. Workers heard strange metallic clanking echoing in the factory. But, skeptics could easily explain the sound of metal could be easily explained in a steel mill. What could not be so easily explained were the moans. Workers reported moans and groans echoing in the building as the ghost of the departed steel worker searched, they said, for his body.

A replacement for the dead worker soon arrived on site. He was brash and brave and certainly didn't believe in ghosts, let alone spirits of steel workers wandering around in search of their body. "Ridiculous," he told his new friends on the job. As a sign of his bravado, he signed up for the late shift, the time when reports of paranormal activity were at its height around the mill.

It was during a late shift that the worker found himself alone on the factory floor. Even for this brave steel worker, he had to admit in his heart of hearts that the atmosphere was eerie. He was quietly finishing up a task when he started to hear strange noises, muffled sounds.

At first, he tried to brush off the noises; after all, it was a loud factory full of equipment capable of producing a wide assortment of bangs, clanks, pings, and knocks.

But the sound grew louder and more persistent. And it sounded like it was coming right for him!

Then he saw it: a shrouded mist floating toward him, making the unmistakable sounds of footsteps! Slowly, deliberately approaching him. As he watched, the misty form became gradually solidified into the form of a worker, who walked down the aisle and suddenly tripped. The ghost fell and then plunged into the bucket of liquefied metal, in a grim reenactment of the accident scene.

The worker, once brave and resolute, shuddered as a scream pierced the empty steel mill floor and echoed down its vast chambers. Then he did what we all would do: he ran out of the mill as an evil laugh followed him.

He never came back. No extra money was worth that.

The ghost, however, stayed, said other workers of the mill.

Most paranormal experts would classify this as a variation of a residual haunting when a spirit reenacts an emotionally charged event in his or her life. It's almost like the psychic energy during a traumatic event etches itself onto the fabric of reality.

With industrial accidents, labor battles, and wars in western Pennsylvania, it's no wonder that residual hauntings are common themes in the paranormal history of Pittsburgh.

The Homestead Police Station, for example, which was studied by the Pittsburgh Paranormal Society, has been rumored to be haunted. Even the officers, who stare down murderers and other ne'er-do-wells on a regular basis, are a bit creeped out by the screams and the unexpected door slams that echo through the headquarters without warning and, more disturbingly, have no natural source. Then there are the reports of a filmy shadow that passes by windows in the building.

But how can an invisible person cast a visible shadow? And how can noises—of door slams and screams—be heard without a source?

The researchers that investigated the Homestead Police Station suggest that the shadows and sounds are the result of a residual haunting, like the tale of the haunted steel worker. Some traumatic event in the police station's past is playing back, like a video on eternal loop that plays over and over again.

But there are other ghost stories that indicate spirits aren't as laid-back and self-absorbed as residual manifestations.

They're called "active haunting" and, as we'll see next, The University of Pittsburgh is a hot spot for tales of active haunting.

Chapter 2

The Cathedral of Haunting

> *Here is eternal spring for you the very stars of heaven are new.*
>
> —Saying on the gates of of the Cathedral of Learning's nave

The University of Pittsburgh began humbly in a log cabin in 1787, although some historians say its origin goes even deeper into the past, back into the 1770's.

Henry Brackenridge, part-educator and part-visionary, founded the Pittsburgh

Academy, which served as the foundation for what would become the University of Pittsburgh. He somehow saw that the lowly log cabin would one day be a great institution and that the small frontier village would one day become one of Pennsylvania's major cities.

"This town in the future must be a place of great manufactory. Indeed the greatest on the continent or the world," Brackenridge said.

That small log cabin now rests, refurbished, in the shadows of Pitt's most famous building, **The Cathedral of Learning**. The Cathedral is a 42-story fulfillment of Brackenridge's prediction about both the city and its namesake University.

Reported to be the second-largest educational building in the world, The Cathedral of Learning was officially opened in 1937 after a nearly decade-long construction project that progressed during the dark depths of the Great Depression. The structure that soars 535 feet above the Oakland neighborhood was more than a college building; it was a symbol. In the words of Pitt Chancellor John Gabbert Bowman:

"The building was to be more than a schoolhouse; it was to be a symbol of the life that Pittsburgh through the years had wanted to live. It was to make visible something of the spirit that was in the hearts of pioneers as, long ago, they sat in their log cabins and thought by candlelight of the great city that would sometime spread out beyond their three rivers and that even they were starting to build."

With respects to Chancellor Bowman, some people say the Cathedral wasn't just a symbol of life, it also become a symbol of death—and what lies beyond.

This Gothic Revival masterpiece is made of steel and limestone and contains approximately 2,000 rooms and more than 2,500 windows!

And a couple of ghosts, too.

The Cathedral of Learning has museum-like rooms dedicated to the cultures that helped build Pittsburgh and its namesake university. One of those rooms on the Cathedral's third floor has been dubbed the Early American Room and one spirit is said to haunt it.

The Early American Room represents life during the 1600s, when Pittsburgh was barely a village and the University of Pittsburgh was just a twinkle in the eye of some founder. A fireplace and all the accoutrement—hooks, kettles, a gridiron, a waffle iron, a bread shovel, and ladles and forks—are on display. Pine beams were brought in from Massachusetts and the dining table and chairs are a stunning example of furniture made from white pine.

Between a blackboard and the fireplace is a secret panel. Once it's unlatched, the wall swings open and a hidden staircase leads to a loft that is furnished as a 17th century bedroom. The bedroom is outfitted with a handmade wedding quilt that experts date to the 1850s. A pine crib is nearby, as are an antique Bible and wash set.

Some paranormal experts say there's a reason that the room is kept so secluded and only accessible through a secret passage. It's haunted. The experts add that there are almost as many ghostly suspects for this haunting as there are floors in this towering tribute to education.

The stories usually filter in from custodians who have the unenviable task of cleaning the strange, secretive room. One custodian said he made his way to the secret room and was horrified to find the quilt folded like someone had just slept—or maybe was sleeping—in the bed. There was even an indentation in the pillow that formed an outline of the head of a human. It wasn't the last time this spectral sleeper visited the bedroom; since then, other visitors have claimed to see the quilt move ever so slightly or have noticed that strange indentation in the blanket and pillow.

The creepy cradle in the Early American Room is another source of haunted tales. Witnesses report walking into the room and seeing the cradle gently rock as though an invisible hand is lulling a child to sleep. You can almost hear the lullaby, they say.

Unseen cradle rockers and phantom nappers are just the beginning of the paranormal phenomena reported in the Nationality Rooms. A tour guide had a run-in with a hungry ghost; or, more accurately, a ghost that made her hungry, in the Early American Room.

While walking through the Early American Room, the guide said she smelled the unmistakable—and delicious—scent of fresh-baked bread. Since there isn't a bakery near the room, nor was there anyone in the room with fresh bread in hand, the guide assumed that the smell was the ghostly remnant of times—perhaps supper times—past.

This scent would probably be classified as a "residual haunting" by most experts. While most residuals are filmy images of ghosts repeating the same actions over and over again, experts suggest that there can also be phantom noises—and even smells.

These are just the first few stories of the Nationality Rooms' haunted history. For over three decades, this space dedicated to exploring the many cultures who call Pittsburgh home has notched up one paranormal encounter after another.

Frequently, students and visitors complained about sudden shifts in temperature as they tour the rooms. There are reports of cold spots—a common sign of spectral guests. In a more dramatic demonstration of supernatural power, one tour group watched in shock as a candle flame inexplicably flared up.

Maybe that will teach them to stop complaining about the cold spots...

It's not just cold spots and paranormal pyrotechnics that send shivers down the spines of guests. Witnesses have claimed to see chilling apparitions of the mysterious entity who has become a permanent resident of the Cathedral of Learning. A psychic visiting the Cathedral said she saw the ghost. She described it as a woman with her hair pulled back and wearing an apron.

A custodian recently described a more frightening encounter with the ghost of the Early American Room. Responsible for cleaning the room and locking the doors, the custodian said he saw a dark shadow near the bed while he climbed the stairs to the room.

"It came out of the room and disappeared in front of me," he told the *Pittsburgh Post Gazette* reporter.

His fellow workers vouch for the custodian's honesty and they say he's telling the truth. One janitor was right behind the man when his co-worker ran into the shadow person. She said the janitor was visibly spooked (literally) and he's difficult to rattle.

Spirit Suspects

Everyone has an opinion about the origin of the Cathedral's haunted activity. For each opinion, there are just as many spirit suspects who are said to be behind the Cathedral's paranormal activity and the ghosts of the Nationality Rooms, specifically.

Events like murders and deadly accidents get blamed for causing most hauntings. But, the Cathedral doesn't have an obvious history of such events. A few paranormal researchers speculate that common everyday objects are the cause of the **Early American Room** haunting. These investigators base this theory on the idea that in most ghost stories, there's a tie between an object and an emotional event or events that create the activity.

The bed, the quilt, and some of the other pieces of furniture on display in the room certainly seem to have a tie with the paranormal action in the Cathedral.

They are original and in their 300-some years of existence may have absorbed their share of trauma and psychic energy, paranormal researchers suggest. According to this haunted object theory, these objects take this energy—and paranormal activity—with them wherever they go.

Oddly enough, the quilt that some say is the source of the haunted activity was passed down to Pitt from the family of Maxine Bruhns, a historian and a leading experts of the Nationality Rooms. Maxine, who serves as the second director of the Nationality Rooms, told the writer in The Original Magazine (a magazine dedicated to Pittsburgh's artists and arts) that the bed has a blanket that was once owned by her West Virginia grandmother, Martha Jane Poe.

It would be ironic justice for Martha, a distant relative of horror master Edgar Allan Poe, to be the source of a haunting and Maxine, for one, believes that it may just be her grandmother that people have sensed and seen in the room.

When she leads tours, she asks visitors to remain quiet and respectful, should the ghost choose to grace them with her presence.

It often works.

Maxine says she has had several encounters with either her grandmother's ghost, or a poltergeist that inhabits the space.

She told the *Pittsburgh Post Gazette* that one time she firmly placed several dried ears of corn on a peg to the left of the fireplace. Without warning or visible cause, the corn exploded off the peg, sending a shower of kernels around the room.

Maxine said the corn was firmly secured on the four-inch nail. And there was no way that an animal could have caused the strange phenomena.

In another incident of possible poltergeist activity, Maxine discovered that the photograph of her grandmother when she was

16 had been cracked, even though the photograph had been carefully packed and stored to prevent just such an accident.

The "corn saga" and cracked photograph—which have become legendary incidents in the Cathedral's extensive paranormal history—are nothing compared to Maxine's next run-in with the spirit of her grandmother.

Maxine said that one night she decided to call her grandmother out and asked her to reveal herself. Her story goes like this:

She was staying overnight in the Nationality Room. (Now there's a brave woman for you.) The room was pitch black and silent. Maxine rolled out her sleeping bag at the foot of the infamous rope bed. Then something moved her to reach out into the unknown.

Into the darkness, Maxine yelled out, "I'm here, Grandma! I'm alone now if you want to contact me."

There was silence at first. But, as Maxine drifted off to sleep, she was awoken by a swishing sound. The noise fluttered by her again!

Was this her grandmother's answer, she wondered.

Then something crashed next to her!

Her bravery seemed to vanish and she laid motionless, too scared to move. Finally, she had the nerve to grab the flashlight and scan the room.

She found that a water bottle she had placed securely in her overnight bag had somehow levitated out of her bag and fallen off the chair.

Maxine did not believe it was an accident or a coincidence.

She yelled out to her grandma again, "Grandma, you can have this damn room!"

While Maxine asks visitors to remain respectful on their tour of the Nationality

Rooms, they should be reminded to keep quiet and respectful throughout the Cathedral because rumor has it the building is packed full of those ghostly presences.

Mary Croghan Schenley

No rest for the romantic

One of the other supernatural presences detected in the Cathedral of Learning is Mary Croghan Schenley. She is said to walk the halls of the Nationality Rooms and maybe even swing off the chandeliers in the ballroom. Once you hear some stories about Mary, you'll realize swinging off the chandeliers isn't out of the question for one of the nation's pioneering party girls.

If you heard the name, "Schenley," it's probably because the name is attached to numerous Pittsburgh landmarks and a few places at the University of Pittsburgh, like Schenley Hall. And, Mary wouldn't have minded at all. She did a pretty good job of spreading the Schenley name around when she was alive.

Mary was the granddaughter and only heir of the vast tracts of land owned by her maternal grandfather and Pittsburgh businessman, James O'Hara. Rich and romantic, she soon made a name for herself in the scandal sheets of her day. As a student at a Staten Island boarding school, Mary fell in love with a 43-year-old British Army captain named, Edward Wyndham Harrington Schenley. They eloped.

Mary was only 15 at the time and a firestorm of disappointment and shame spread across the Atlantic as the couple sought refuge in England. To make matters worse, this was the third elopement for the good captain.

Mary's rich father threatened to cut his daughter off entirely if she went through with the marriage.

Luckily, the third time would be a charm for the captain and his young, wealthy bride.

After the couple fell on hard times, Mary's father had a change of heart and accepted his daughter back into the family fold (and back into the inheritance). Schenley lived most of her life in London, but was generous with the loads of money and land she inherited back in America. Most of the land was donated to Pittsburgh, its churches, institutions, and schools, including the University of Pittsburgh and the plot of land that the Cathedral now rests on.

Is Mary's vivacious spirit prompting the Cathedral's haunting? Maybe. But there are more theories to examine.

Another legend is that objects in the Croghan-Schenley Ballroom in the Cathedral of Learning are causing the Cathedral's haunting.

The ballroom is located on the first floor and, like the rest of the Cathedral, has its share of mysteries. For instance, the room has a hidden passageway in the fireplace that connects it with the adjoining Oval Room. The rooms were originally part of William Croghan

Jr.'s mansion, but were painstakingly removed and restored in the cathedral when a demolition project threatened to level the mansion.

Life Magazine actually featured the story about the restoration project in a 1945 edition. The title of the article, ominously enough, was "Life Visits a Haunted House."

However, the chandeliers draw most of the supernatural attention.

The refurbished rooms are dominated by a hand-cut glass chandelier. The chandelier, which also reportedly hung in Mary's own mansion, is an amazingly ornate piece. It's also amazingly haunted. Witnesses have seen the chandelier begin to shake. At other times, it sways. There is no breeze, these witnesses say. Nor does there seem to be any vibrations causing the disturbance—at least, vibrations of the mundane, earthly sort. If there is a vibration, it doesn't disturb any of the other objects in the room. Witnesses say that even when they see the chandelier sway, they notice that papers don't flutter, hair doesn't blow, and the furniture remains in place.

At other times, Mary engages in some of her own restoration efforts.

In one of the more extreme examples of paranormal activity in the Cathedral of Learning, the beds have been unmade and the furniture has been rearranged, even though the night crew had locked all the doors. Members of the terrified day crew who have witnessed the odd redecoration efforts claim there is no natural explanation for the actions that include dramatic moves of large, heavy objects and furniture.

There's a debate among the paranormal community and those who study folklore at Pitt. Some say Mary, alone, is the sole ghost involved in the Nationality Rooms' paranormal reputation, but others say she's just one of the spirits.

It might not have anything to do with old quilts or swinging chandeliers, say other students familiar with the haunting of the skyscraping cathedral; it might be that the ghost in the Early American room needs a drink to wash down all that fresh-baked bread.

Wandering Soul Food
The Cathedral's creepy cafeteria

Ever since John Belushi screamed the immortal words, "food fight," and chucked his plate of food across the cafeteria room, college food has been the stuff of both legend and derision.

The problem at the Cathedral of Learning isn't bad food, or food fights. By all accounts, the food in the cathedral gets rave reviews. There's even a sushi bar! There doesn't seem to be a tradition of tossing food at your cafeteria mates, either.

The cooks and workers don't seem to be the cause of any trouble. They get kudos from diners, too.

The problem with grabbing a bite to eat at one of the food establishments in the Cathedral is the spirit visitors who frequent the building and freak out students and workers on a regular occasion.

The Cathedral's cafeteria is just one more haunted hot spot in the building, according to several accounts. Workers in the cafeteria are among the primary witnesses who tell stories of strange activity in the cafeteria. And they're not just talking about the unusual activity of some of the students who are part of the late-night crowd.

These strange happenings usually occur at night and usually when the cafeteria is dead—so to speak. At the top of the supernatural menu at the cafeteria is a heaping-helping of poltergeist activity. Witnesses have seen carts start to move by themselves—on a perfectly level floor, they add. Then, there are tales of boxes that get pushed along the floor, or spin suddenly and inexplicably.

The roving carts and boxes seem to be directed by an unseen force.

It could be the same force that workers sense walking by them late at night. It's an eerie feeling, they say, not like a breeze or a wind. It's an feeling like someone, or something, passing so close you can feel their presence.

And sometimes, the workers report, this presence passes right through you.

One more sign of ghostly activity in the cafeteria has been reported by more than a couple of students and workers. It's a chilling reminder of the spirit world that haunts the Cathedral. Witnesses have seen the handle of an ice machine suddenly depress and splatter ice cubes all over the floor.

While cynics quickly point out that a faulty ice machine could cause the spill, a few reports indicate that people have seen the handle actually move, like some invisible force was pushing it.

Seeking Answers in the Cathedral of the Unknown

Education, which the Cathedral of Learning represents in all of its sky-topping, 42-story glory, is a gateway for those seeking answers and for those who wish to explore the unknown. These seekers—teachers and students—are bound and determined to explore all those areas that were once objects of both fear and curiosity, from the depths of the earth to the unfathomable stretches of deep space.

This desire to explore led to "science"— a rigorous, methodical examination of the unknown.

But, there's one source of the unknown that appears safely tucked away from the powerful punches of science and education: that mysterious field where life settles after death. There are those who walk on the Pitt campus who have a solution—ignore it. If science can't measure it, it doesn't exist. They don't believe in ghosts or spirits. Poltergeists have a natural explanation. End of story.

But, for others, it's the accounts of ghostly visitors and unexplained phenomena of the unknown that echo from the Cathedral of Learning and other parts of the University that make ignoring the unknown impossible for others.

Cafeteria workers, custodians, curators, and students who have spent nights in the long, dark halls of the Cathedral of Learning have an answer to skeptics: spend a night in the Cathedral.

Spending some time at night in this Cathedral of the Unknown, they say, is a life changing and possibly even a death-altering experience.

Chapter 3

Alumni Hall

Pitt's version of the Da Vinci Code?

Alumni Hall was not always a temple in the pantheon of higher education.

It has a more mystical origin.

In the early days of the 20th century, the imposing limestone building that rests on Fifth Avenue at Pitt was used as a Masonic Temple. Masons, if you follow the reams of conspiracy theories, did not just possess the secrets of building, they possessed the secrets of magic.

These secrets are passed on to members and followers through Masonic rituals. These powerful rituals were once performed in Alumni Hall. Students now wonder if the residual magic left over from those days as a hall of secret rites and rituals is now causing Alumni Hall's current haunted activity.

Pitt purchased the building in the early 1990s. Alumni Hall, a massive structure with an extended base, is highlighted with some impressive architectural features, like the ornamental terra cotta pediment and clay tile roof that make the building look like a classic temple.

Pitt transformed Masonic Temple through extensive renovations into a veritable temple of Pitt glory. The building was eventually added as a historic landmark to the Pittsburgh History and Landmark Foundation's list of such structures in the city.

The Pitt Alumni Association, which now makes its home in the building, is the official keeper of the gloried past of Pitt's many alumni standouts. The Legacy Gallery in Alumni Hall, currently housed on the first floor, offers interactive kiosks for people to explore alumni, faculty, and student achievements.

The virtual archive, which serves as an electronic exploration into Pitt's history and history-makers, isn't the only reminder of the past. According to reports, several witnesses have seen a ghost in Alumni Hall.

Most stories about the Alumni Hall ghost come from folks who were walking through the building after hours or before the mad rush of workers and visitors who arrive each morning. Witnesses, who are usually alone, say they're walking down the silent, empty halls when they see a figure out of the corner of their eyes.

The ghost has been described as a man clad in a black tuxedo. (There must be formal occasions in the afterlife.) The man emerges from a shadowy corner and heads toward one of the stairwells. His gait has been described as an eerie glide, not a walk.

Most witnesses report being so stunned that they can't move. Only the truly brave follow the man. According to one story, a witness chased after the figure and said the ghost faded away as he walked down the steps. And disappeared.

So, who is this impeccably-attired spirit?

No one knows.

He doesn't seem to resemble any of the officials, administrators, legendary sports heroes, or other people from Pitt's past who might want to continue to linger around the alumni headquarters.

The figure doesn't look like any of past Pittsburgh's famous historic figures, either. He doesn't resemble Andrew Carnegie, or Henry Clay Frick, or Thomas Mellon, or Charles Schwab, or other Pittsburgh pioneers.

Experts of Pittsburgh's paranormal heritage have one guess, though: they believe this well-dressed spirit is the ghost of a lost Mason. Perhaps, he's trapped between the world of the living and the world of the dead. Or, maybe he's a little confused that his Masonic Temple has been renovated into a modern alumni facility.

Or is this spirit just one more secret that the ancient order of Masons refuses to divulge?

Chapter 4

Bruce Hall

Residence life meets resident after life.

Dormitories are a home-away-from-home for thousands of Pitt students.

They're also the home base of some of Pitt's most famous paranormal outbreaks.

Bruce Hall leads the way in non-living residence life. The dorm is considered one of the most haunted spots on campus.

It's so haunted that one of the staff's holiday traditions is to hang out a stocking for each of the dorm's employees. They even make sure that there's a stocking for Harriet. Although she shows up quite regularly, Harriet isn't really a Pitt employee. In fact, she's not even really alive.

Harriet is the name that students and staff have given to the ghost who supposedly haunts the mysterious Bruce Hall.

Bruce Hall is named after former chancellor Robert Bruce. Bruce is regarded as the first chancellor of Pitt, even though it was named Western University of Pennsylvania at the time.

One of Bruce's famous students included Thomas Mellon, who founded the Mellon financial empire. Mellon remembered Bruce fondly in his autobiography:

"He was highly cultured in general literature, an extensive reader, liberal minded, and a most accurate scholar in the several branches he professed. He had all the philosophy of Bacon and Descartes, Hume, Reid, and Dugald Stewart at command—he had himself been a student of Dugald Stewart."

Bruce Hall, on Fifth Avenue, is part of the Schenley Quad, a section of Pitt with eight residence halls, and was once called the Schenley Apartments. And, of course, the Schenley name has been associated with several other Pitt hauntings, including the ghosts that stalk the University's soaring Cathedral of Learning.

Even though the staff and students of Bruce Hall dubbed the ghost, Harriet, there's still a bit of confusion as to who is really behind the hauntings. We can't be sure the ghost is male or female. Or, that it's even a ghost, or a poltergeist.

Whatever the origin, one story about the Bruce Hall haunting goes like this:

When it was an apartment building, the owner or caretaker (the reports vary) lived on the 12th floor. For several years, he had been involved in an affair, at least that's one version of the story.

One of the people involved in this love triangle committed suicide. The story varies here, too. In some reports, the wife committed suicide; in others, the mistress takes her own life. There are even other stories that indicate that the husband, upset by the shame he brought on his family, kills himself. Most reports say that the suicide occurred in the stairwell.

The tales of the love-triangle-gone bad do agree on one thing: a spirit has unfinished business in Bruce Hall.

No one knows exactly when the spirit encounters started in Bruce Hall, but the stories of something amiss in the building were circulated before it became a dorm. So, we can't just blame the exuberance of college kids for the stories.

A few Schenley Apartment dwellers say they saw a spirit wandering the stairwell of the building. Tales of paranormal events filtered out, too. Residents would come home and find tables and chairs moved, even though apartment rooms were locked tight. Renters blamed the managers, or employees, for sneaking into rooms, even as management protested that they—or their workers—had nothing to do with the sudden redecoration efforts in the apartments.

No one knows whether the University knew they were buying haunted goods when they turned the apartment building into residence halls. But the stories didn't disappear when the lease was signed.

In fact, the tales of something mysterious and spooky haunting Bruce Hall grew at a torrid pace when the University assumed ownership.

Bruce Hall's Banquet Hall is a prime haunting location.

You may, after this story, be able to detect a theme among Pitt haunts. The ghosts at Pitt are foodies. Like the spirit, or spirits, who haunt the Cathedral of Learning, a few spooks like to visit the banquet room in Bruce Hall. Over the years, workers have claimed to witness a series of strange events that convinced them that a spirit was present.

One of the reports centers on the doors of the cabinets that are used for storage. People say these doors inexplicably open—and close. At other times, the cabinets just rattle.

One witness said that each time the workers left the room, they heard a sharp "bang" of a cabinet door. When the workers returned, the room was eerily still and silent. Despite the stillness and no sign of human intervention, the now freaked-out banquet workers say they still felt a presence was watching over them.

Could it be that Harriet was an unhappy banquet manager during her former life? The ghost seems to be particularly concerned about table settings, much to the frustration of the staff's current banquet organizers.

If the table isn't set just so, Harriet apparently tosses napkins on the floor, workers say. Skeptics easily dismiss this manifestation as a practical joker on the staff, or blame it on a random gust of breeze, but workers say those explanations can't explain away the strange activity. They point out that other napkins aren't disturbed, even though they are in the direct path of the phantom breeze and no one has ever admitted to pulling a prank.

Banquet workers at Pitt are meticulous about their work. One might say they're so meticulous at making everything look so perfect that they could use some counseling. Maybe Harriet knows the staff's little compulsive tendencies and, just to get on their nerves, she jumbles up the place settings. Workers say they've discovered spoons and forks moved around.

Harriet, or whoever the ghost of the banquet hall is, may or may not be the same spook roaming Bruce Hall's 12th floor. If it is the same, Harriet's behavior in other parts of Bruce Hall is much more intense. Students have reported sounds in the stairwell, like someone walking—or running—up and down the steps. The same sound of frantic footwork echoes through the 12th floor. But, when witnesses peak around the corner to see who's making the racket, there's nobody there.

Some witnesses also report hearing a voice—a woman's voice—echoing in the same stairwell.

Could these be the spirit reminders of the tragic love triangle, as some students speculate?

The elevator is another hot spot for paranormal activity in the building, witnesses say. More than one unsuspecting rider has jumped on the elevator and ended up taking a ride into the twilight zone. They report that, despite the buttons they push, the elevator automatically deposits them on Bruce Hall's haunted 12th floor. One visitor said the elevator stopped at the 12th floor and then refused to budge—either up or down—until she wisely made a break for it. She jumped out of the elevator and headed to the stairwell. Unfortunately for her, she soon found out that the 12th floor stairwell is haunted, too. As she walked down the steps, she heard those famous footsteps. At first, she thought the sounds were nothing more than an echo of her own footsteps. So, she stopped.

And the sound of footsteps kept coming. Closer. The sounds echoed out a few flights above her.

She immediately picked up the pace and ran to the exit.

After this escape from Bruce Hall's cursed elevator, she made a quick exit from the building and entered into Bruce Hall's haunted history.

Chapter 5

The Ghost of Lillian Russell

I am haunted, hear me roar

Pitt's campuses are known for their strong women. The University's female students were—and are—in the forefront of the push for equality and justice.

Maybe that's why strong female presences make up the lion's (or panther's) share of the appearance in Pitt's paranormal lore. There's Madame Schenley in the Cathedral of Learning. Harriet uses her womanly wiles to give Bruce Hall's guests and workers the willies.

Another example of female haunting on Pitt's main campus occurs at the William Pitt Union, once called the Schenley Hotel. It also just happens to be the site of one of Pitt's most famous—or infamous—celebrity ghosts, too.

Lillian Russell wasn't a native Pittsburgher. She was born in Iowa and raised in Chicago—and then she raised hell everywhere else.

According to *the New York Times*, Russell and Alexander Pollock Moore were married in the Schenley Hotel, the future William Pitt Union building. A church wedding could not be arranged due to, perhaps, Russell's extensive love and marriage resume. A few experts of paranormal Pitt wonder whether the emotions—both positive and negative—that swirled around during the wedding might be a reason why Lillian's spirit remains anchored in the building.

It fits Lillian's life story. She was definitely a powerful spirit, a spirit that marched—and continues to march in the after life—to the beat of a different drummer.

When her parents separated, she moved to New York with her mother and began her professional singing career. Starting with roles in comic operas, Lillian quickly rose through the ranks of the most sought-after actresses in the Big Apple. She married a composer named

Edward Solomon. He was arrested for bigamy and the marriage quickly dissolved.

It was the first of four whirlwind marriages, although her most famous liaison wasn't a marriage at all. She had been the long-time companion of the one and only Diamond Jim Brady, a financier and stock market master. They were a great match, people said. They both had voracious appetites for life and, at least according to people who saw the couple at dinner, they both had voracious appetites period.

Eventually, though, Lillian's relationship with Diamond Jim broke up and she fell for a Pittsburgh newspaper (*The Pittsburgh Leader*) owner. The marriage came at an opportune time for ever-opportunistic Lillian. Her singing and dramatic career was starting to fade and she started to write newspaper columns.

She was able to use *the Leader* as a platform of some of her favorite causes: women's rights, suffrage, and self-help.

Lillian died in Pittsburgh on June 6, 1922 at the age of 61. She had just returned home from a fact-finding mission on immigration policy for President Warren Harding.

The famous diva was buried in Allegheny Cemetery in Pittsburgh. But her spirit has never left.

Since her death, a steady stream of stories have passed on about a wandering spirit who stalked the corridors of William Pitt Union Hall, especially on the building's 4th floor, the same floor where Lillian lived during a stretch of her earthly existences and where the "Lillian Russell Room" is currently situated. People have witnessed the apparition of a woman on that floor. The description of the ghost's clothes and hairstyle sounds uncannily like someone from the early 20th century. And uncannily like a description of the one-and-only Lillian Russell.

Other strange activity has been reported in the Lillian Russell Room. Someone—or something—reportedly moves objects and rearranges furniture. Perhaps creepiest of all, other witnesses say they get a weird feeling in the room—like unseen eyes are constantly watching them.

That would be a little ironic: after years of having the eyes of adoring, anonymous fans on her, Lillian Russell now has her eyes on the thousands of Pitt students who enter the William Pitt Union Building.

The ghost of Lillian Russell has some celebrity company in the William Pitt Union Building. One student legend centers on a pretty ballerina, who now serves as a warning to slumbering students.

According to the tale, when the Russian National Ballet took residence at the Schenley Hotel during a series of performances at Pittsburgh, the prima ballerina for the troupe was having a little trouble keeping her eyes open. Days of travel and the grueling performances finally took a toll on the dancer. She fell asleep before the performance and was late. In truth, she had already been skating on thin ice, or dancing on tip toes, as the case may be. A young, ambitious understudy was eagerly waiting in the wings.

The understudy took full advantage of the opportunity. She wowed the crowd of Pittsburgh dance aficionados and, more importantly, she wowed the company's director, who now believed that it was time to replace the more experienced, more expensive ballerina. When the ballerina received news that she was let go, she became so distraught that she killed herself.

The ghost of this dancer now reportedly haunts the **Transky Family Lounge**.

Another unverified legend has been told about this Grande Dame of the Dance. One report states that if a Pitt student falls asleep in the lounge, the ghost of the ballerina will wake him or her up just in time to make the next class or appointment. This ghost, it seems, doesn't cause alarm, she acts as an alarm, ensuring that the Pitt students don't succumb to her unpunctual fate.

Chapter 6

Other Pittsburgh Higher Ed Haunts
Encountering more ghosts in the hallowed halls of paranormal Pittsburgh

The University of Pittsburgh is just one of the haunted hot spots in the city. But Pittsburgh is the home base for lots of colleges and universities that have their own ghostly legacy. Poltergeists, ghosts, and spirits have applied for admission at these schools, too.

In this chapter, we'll explore tales and legends about some of Pittsburgh's other collegiate ghosts.

Byers Hall CCAC
Community College of Allegheny County

The Byers Mansion was built by iron baron Alexander Byers on Pittsburgh's famous Millionaire's Row in 1898. The majestic building became a bit of a sensation in the city. It was beautifully furnished and filled with decorations and antiques. And ghosts.

One of the saddest and most tragic tales of Pittsburgh's paranormal victims centers on Alexander's daughter and granddaughter. His daughter lived in the mansion and left her own daughter in the care of a nanny.

While the nanny took a nap, the daughter somehow crawled onto a skylight. The skylight crashed down and the fall killed the four-year-old.

Distraught, the nanny immediately hanged herself. The nanny—or someone— etched the words "don't blame me" in dust.

One super-creepy detail about the suicide still shocks. According to the tale, when the first people found the body of the nanny they also saw the ghost of the little girl watching the body swing from the noose.

Ever since the incident, there have been more stories of strange goings-on in the mansion. Those stories did not abate when the mansion was refurbished as an administrative building and student union for the Community College of Allegheny County (CCAC).

In fact, the stories of ghostly encounters in the building accelerated after the renovation. The tales of spirits went viral.

The ghost of the little girl was seen at various spots throughout the mansion.

In the afterlife, the child and the nanny who neglected her have reconciled. They're seen running up the steps together.

There are other, more ominous messages from the beyond, though. Sometimes, for example, a thud—like the sound of a body dropping from a noose—is heard in the building. People have also discovered the haunting message, "don't blame me," written in dust around the Byers Mansion.

Interestingly, the school finally replaced the skylight. Those students who are more conspiracy-minded believe that the school removed the skylight to exorcise the ghost. If so, it seems to have worked. The ghost of the girl is seen less frequently.

But, the ill-fated nanny doesn't seem to want to leave just yet. Students say she continues to haunt the halls, looking for her escape from her eternal, self-imposed punishment.

Carlow University

Carlow University is one of Pittsburgh's most famous Catholic universities. Although it's primarily a school for women, the university did allow men in shortly after World War II.

When Carlow began admitting ghosts and spirits is anyone's guess.

But, the University now has earned a reputation of being another one of the Pittsburgh area's spooky spots. A misty apparition has been seen around campus. Students also have complained that they are startled out of their sleep by scratching sounds that seems to emanate from within the walls. That's typical behavior of a poltergeist. Or a malicious entity.

Other poltergeist phenomena have been reported at Carlow. Lights turn on an off— apparently all by themselves.

What isn't clear is the source of the haunting. One theory: the bizarre behavior is the ghost of a former female student who is upset by the inclusion of messy men into the formerly all-female Carlow University.

Chatham College

Chatham College could never compete with Pitt in athletics. But, when it comes to paranormal activity, Chatham gives Pittsburgh's biggest university a run for its supernatural money.

The scenic campus rests in the Shadyside section of "the burgh" and is dotted with buildings that students and faculty say are haunted. Really haunted. Phenomena range from poltergeist activity to the haunting, mournful cries of children.

While most school administrators in other universities try to hide their campuses' haunted legacies, Chatham embraces it, even hosting ghost walks around Halloween. And there's a lot to tour.

One of Chatham's most famous haunted buildings on the tour is the Mellon Hall. The former home of Andrew Mellon, once the Secretary of Treasury, is used as the administrative building.

When Mellon acquired the property he installed a bowling alley and an indoor swimming pool. Even though the pool is no longer in use, the features act as a magnet for paranormal powers, according to one legend about the property.

People say they have heard two voices—possibly the voices of Mellon and industrialist Henry Frick—talking while they listen to music. Others smell cigar smoke wafting through the halls. Creepy stories about the bowling alley have been collected over the years, too. The pins re-set all by themselves.

Another sure-fire sign of paranormal activity—dipping room temperatures—are reported in the Mellon Center, too.

Fickes Hall Spooks

Another famous haunted building at Chatham is Fickes Hall. It was once the home of Edwin Stanton Fickes, an industrialist and executive for ALCOA. Fickes is also the prime suspect for the strange events that happen at the dorm.

Students report that when they come back to their locked rooms, someone has rummaged through the place. Desk drawers are opened and closets have been disturbed. But there's no sign of any human intervention. There's nothing stolen and there's no sign of a break-in.

Some students have even reported they felt an eerie presence crawl onto the bed while they were sleeping, or, at least, while they were trying to sleep.

Another rumor is that a woman committed suicide in the building and her spirit roams the halls on the first floor. Even though there doesn't seem to be any historical evidence or newspaper accounts of that tragedy, the legend continues to be passed on—class after class.

On the third floor, there are more stories of tragic spirits. In one tale, a boy reportedly fell out of a window. His ghost has also been seen and heard in Fickes Hall.

Berry Hall

Once a dorm for Chatham students and now the admissions office, Berry Hall is filled with the echoes of its haunted past.

When it was a dorm, students said they could hear the cries of children. A quick inspection would reveal, obviously, there were no kids present in the dormitory at the time.

These sad criess could be attributed to what paranormal researchers call residual phenomena. When emotions are intense, this psychic energy can etch its presence onto the fabric of reality like grooves in a record. This energy then replays in an infinite loop. In the case of Berry Hall, people say children died due to some unrecorded incident in the building. The fear and grief—as well as the grief of their parents—has created a sonic reminder of the pain that is heard over and over again.

Duquesne University

There are a few ghosts roaming around the buildings of one of Pitt's closest higher education rivals, Duquesne University.

One legend is that Old Main, a building on the Duquesne campus, was used as a stopping point on the Underground Railroad, a way that slaves traveled through the north to freedom. The story says that you can hear moans and chatting of people in the basement. The suggestion is that these sounds are, like the children crying in Berry Hall, the audible remnants of those intrepid freedom seekers.

In addition to the sounds of haunting, there are frequent visual cues of ghostly activity. Witnesses say objects move all by themselves and lights turn on and off.

St. Ann's Living Learning Center is another haunted spot on the Duquesne University campus. The ghost of a boy reportedly roams the halls of this building.

Chapter 7

Pitt's Haunted Branch Campuses

With Pitt's growing reputation as an academic and athletic leader in Pennsylvania education, the number of eager students who wanted to apply to the University of Pittsburgh outstripped the number of seats available at the University's Pittsburgh-based campus. This accelerating demand spurred University leaders to create regional campuses throughout Pennsylvania.

Over time, Pitt built four of these learning centers around the state: Bradford (in northern Pennsylvania), Greensburg, Johnstown, and Titusville.

Besides reaching the potential students geographically, the campuses were designed to reach them academically. It's no easy task to transition from high school to college; nor is it an easy transition for students who will move from the largely rural areas of the Keystone state to Pitt's urban campus. Pitt designed these branch campuses as a way to introduce new students to the rigors of University scholarship.

However, there is one thing that students at Pitt's branch campuses don't need a refresher course on if and when they traveled to Pittsburgh: the paranormal.

It turns out that these branch campuses have spooky stories about haunted buildings and scary spots all of their own.

From haunted cemeteries to caves inhabited by giants, and from ghost towns to spirit-infested mansions, Pitt's branch campuses are ghost-for-ghost equal to the big city campus.

We'll start our journey into these supernatural branch campuses with a trip to Pitt's top (at least geographically speaking) campus in Bradford.

Chapter 8

Bradford

Pitt-Bradford is the northernmost Pitt campus.

The town of Bradford and the surrounding region is almost a direct opposite of Pitt's bustling, urban Pittsburgh campus. Situated at the top of Pennsylvania and thickly surrounded by the Allegheny National Forest, Pitt-Bradford is a calm, serene place.

The campus offers students more than 40 majors and over 50 minors. Pitt-Bradford students often say they picked the Bradford campus because the site's scenic beauty and quiet makes the rigors of studying a little easier. It's probably fair to say that Bradford has less to tempt the wavering attention span of a student like the bright city lights of Pittsburgh.

Bradford may be a long way from oil rich Texas, but at one time the rugged McKean

County town at the northern reaches of Pennsylvania's wilderness was an oil boom town.

    In the late 1800s, a high-grade crude oil was discovered near Bradford. And the rush was on to make money from this black gold.

    Overnight, the little town in the Allegheny Forest boomed into a small city. Oil-seekers and land speculators came to Bradford. Derricks were constructed and oil wells were drilled. Refineries and other oil service installations were hastily built. Businesses bloomed in the once-desolate speck of forest.

    But just because civilization was ready to make its home in the thick wilderness, the wilderness was not ready to totally give up its domain to civilization. Spooky legends circulated—and continue to circulate—among the enterprising men and women of Bradford about the strange, almost mystical powers that stalk the deep reaches of the forests that surrounded their quaint, but thriving community.

By 1963, the boom days were over for Bradford and the region confronted a problem.

With the lack of industry and educational facilities, students left town for other universities when they graduated. Some went to Penn State. Others traveled north to New York schools. Another group made the trek to Pittsburgh to attend the University of Pittsburgh.

To stop this brain drain, the people of Bradford pushed for a Pitt campus.

The campus started out small when Dr. Donald E. Swarts, former dean of Pitt-Johnstown, was named the fledgling campus's first president. The first building they bought was called the Hampsher House, a building once owned by the Bradford Hospital. They revamped the building to make way for classrooms, a library, and student lounges and study facilities.

The two-year college welcomed about 143 full-time students and 145 part-time students.

Creating a Pitt campus in Bradford spawned a renewed flourish of civilization in the community and focused the light of icy scientific rationality on the old Boomtown and its legends. But, try as it might, science never dispelled the haunted legends and creepy tales that lurked in the thickly-timbered mountains just beyond the gates of the campus.

Students still pass around tales of Bradford's haunted mountains and the very bravest students often travel to this wide swath of timber called the Allegheny National Forest to investigate reports of ghosts, monsters, and UFOs first-hand.

The Forest of Mystery

The epicenter for paranormal activity near Bradford is the Kinzua Dam. It has been that way for as long as the ancient people who inhabited this land can remember.

Vast and thickly-forested, the area that surrounds the Kinzua Dam was sacred to the Seneca Indian tribes.

And now it's cursed.

The curse supposedly started when President John F. Kennedy unleashed occult forces when he ordered the building of the Kinzua Dam in 1960. The move violated a treaty the stretched back for centuries between William Penn and Chief Cornplanter that guaranteed this sacred spot would be preserved for the Seneca nation.

Besides breaking this oath, the dam project itself may have unleashed angry spirits. The water from the newly-built dam washed over a graveyard for Native Americans. Even though officials tried to appease the spirits by transporting the bones to a safer spot, the tear in the fabric between the living and the dead had formed, according to paranormal experts.

That's when sightings of spirits became more frequent.

Several witnesses said they saw the filmy presence of what looked like an Indian maiden floating over the Allegheny Reservoir, the huge body of water created by the dam. It's a matter of debate among the paranormal research community just who this spirit is. It could be a protective spirit that is upset about the disturbance on sacred tribal land. Another camp believes she is the spirit of one of the dead Seneca maidens who once rested peacefully in the cemetery.

Pitt students can find more paranormal activity in the area. A host of tales and legends lurk in the Allegheny Reservoir and the mountains that surround it.

The lake is widely reported to contain the Keystone state's version of the Loch Ness Monster. Fishing enthusiasts, who are themselves lured to the lakes and streams by tales of the big fish that inhabit the waters, have claimed to run into a trophy-sized aquatic animal that they never expected.

A horned sea creature has been spotted in the lake. The appearances are brief and the animal quickly disappears when approached and, to be honest, not too many anglers are brave enough to get a closer look.

Not too far from the dam is another site for the Pitt campus's paranormal buffs. It's a majestic sweep of the Allegheny River that bends around a deep cut of the mountains. Tall, rock cliffs tower over the site.

Some say it's not just the cliffs that tower over the river.

While working on the Kinzua Dam, a group of quarry workers reportedly uncovered a cave. Not necessarily an unusual thing for quarry workers to do, but this cave appeared to once have been inhabited—by giants. The discovery of huge stone tools synched up with Native American legends of a race of giants that lived in the region.

The area of the discovery was known as Big Bend. It, apparently, wasn't just the bend in the river that was so big.

After the discovery, other stories began to pop up about a race of giants who once lived in the area and left their artifacts. It even led to a legend that makes the Kinzua dam area sound like it's Pennsylvania's Area 51.

The story, related on the web site of the Paranormal Ghost Society, starts with a military convoy arriving stealthily in the area and making their way toward the cave area. It's not an easy hike.

Witnesses later reported that hearing a shoot out of some kind.

Then the soldiers left the area—in a hurry. You might say that "retreated" would be a better word. The military convoy was packed up and the vehicles sped through the towns that surround the Allegheny Forest.

Was it simply a military exercise?

If it was, the military never told the press that an exercise was scheduled.

Conspiracy theorists have another reason. The military ran into the supernatural forces that inhabit the forces. The theorists, themselves, though are split. There are those that suggest the soldiers were called in after an encounter with an alien craft that landed near Big Bend. Others say the team met up with the giants of Allegheny Forest.

Chapter 9

Johnstown, the City That Beat Death

"And now begins the task of burying the dead and caring for the living. It is Wednesday morning. Scarcely has daylight broken before a thousand funerals are in progress on the green hillsides. There were no hearses, few mourners, and as little solemnity as formality. The majority of the coffins were of rough pine. The pall-bearers were strong ox-teams, and instead of six pallbearers to one coffin, there were generally six coffins to one-team. Silently the processions moved, and silently they unloaded their burdens in the lap of mother earth. No minister of God was there to pronounce a last blessing as the clods rattled down, except a few faithful priests who had followed some representatives of their faith to the grave."

—History of the Johnstown Flood, by Willis Fletcher Johnson, 1889

Johnstown, a city of 26,000 people that rests about 60 miles east of Pittsburgh, is host to University of Pitt at Johnstown. It's also host to its share of restless spirits.

The city of Johnstown is one of the few places that managed to turn a disaster into a tourist attraction.

Johnstown sits, like a bucket, in a valley completely surrounded by towering mountains. In 1889, the city paid dearly for this topographical anomaly.

During a spell of heavy May rains in 1889, the nearby South Fork Dam collapsed. A wall of water, picking up trees, houses, trains, metal, and other debris, followed the natural contours of the earth and crashed headlong into the city. The flood and fires that followed killed thousands of citizens and spawned dozens of legends about spirits and ghosts around Johnstown.

The South Fork dam is a spiritual epicenter.

Another favorite haunt in the Johnstown area is the Stone Bridge. According to historical accounts, a thirty-foot pile of debris jammed up against the Stone Bridge beneath the South Fork Dam.

When the bridge eventually broke, the rush of water—picking up trees, pieces of homes, train cars, and barbed wire—rushed into the valley, like a tsunami from hell. To complete the hellish effect, the oil that spilled into the flooding waters caught on fire.

The bodies were washed away. Some were never recovered. But residents also say that their souls continue to live on. There are even reports of desperate cries of "help" cascading down the valley from the infamous spot of the Stone Bridge.

Out of the Ashes...

If the story of that 1889 flood was one of Pennsylvania's most tragic tales, accounts of how Johnstown rebuilt was one the state's most heroic moments. Not only did the town rebuild, but the flood recovery effort became a rallying point for the city's resourcefulness and hardiness, a legacy that helped them through future upheavals, like the loss of the steel and coal industries. The Johnstown area even created a tourist industry out of the event, attracting thousands of tourist each year who are interested in seeing the site of the Great Flood, visiting the Flood Museum, and catching sight of some of the ghosts that haunt the city.

A dramatic example of Johnstown's ability to survive disaster and reinvent itself is the campus of the University of Pitt-Johnstown, better known as UPJ. The campus that was established in Johnstown in 1927 was one of the first examples of a regional campus.

In the early 1960s, the campus was moved to Richland Township, a Johnstown that would give the school more room to grow. By 1967, the campus included two classroom buildings, dormitories, and a student union. Over the years, it's grown considerably. And so have reports of paranormal encounters.

Native School Spirits

The Pitt campus at Johnstown reflects the town's spooky tradition and may even rival its big brother campus in Pittsburgh, at least in the number of rumors of hauntings and supernatural activity.

Strangely, few of the UPJ ghosts are apparently connected with the floods. Students claim that the eerie happenings at the school are caused by the site's unique location.

The campus, they say, is built on sacred ground.

Legend has it that the campus rests on ground that indigenous people considered sacred and that Native American graves were disturbed during the construction of several campus buildings.

This is a paranormal no-no.

There's evidence that lends credence to this theory. Shawnee and Delaware tribes were active in western Pennsylvania and had settlements near Johnstown. Experts of these indigenous cultures have identified burial mounds in the region, as well. (The mound at a nearby site, called Fort Hill, is perhaps the most famous example of an area burial mound.)

Campus paranormal theorists say there were Indian mounds on campus. But, these mounds were removed to make way for UPJ.

If it is true, it could explain the paranormal activity on the school's athletic fields. For most colleges, a rowdy, cheering student section creates a home field advantage, called school spirit. UPJ takes it one step beyond, bolstering school spirit with actual spirits.

The soccer field has earned a particular reputation for being haunted by the ghosts of Native Americans. Students claim to hear weird noises that drift in the wind over the fields and feel unseen presences on the athletic fields.

There are those who say, if you listen closely, you'll realize that the noise isn't a noise, at all. It's the sound of Native American spirits singing. Perhaps it's just residual energy of the tribes that's trapped on the campus. Or, maybe these voices are raising songs of lament, crying for the land they once owned.

Haunted Dorms

Those eerie melodies of the area's first inhabitants—and perhaps their spirits—drift off the athletic fields and into some of the nearby buildings, too, students report.

Oak Hall and Laurel Hall, which are nestled in these reportedly haunted woods, are the sites of several campus ghost tales. The dorms, like the athletic field, are supposedly built directly on sacred territory.

During the night, people claim to hear drumming erupting from the woods that surround the dorms. And, to the best of the students' collective knowledge, the marching band doesn't practice in the wee hours of the morning. Most say this is the drumming of the native spirits displaced by the campus construction project.

Only the brave walk across that sliver of land that separates the dorms at night when this ghostly drumming is heard.

But, even the solid walls of the dorm form no protection against these restless spirits. Paranormal activity has been reported in both buildings. Apparitions have been spotted in the residence halls and objects have been seen moving all by themselves.

The incidents occurred so frequently—and became so creepy—that at least one group of students banded together to rid their temporary homes of their permanent otherwordly residences. (After all, they weren't chipping in on food and utilities.) Using common ghost-busting techniques, they tried to exorcise the ghost—or ghosts—in the dorm.

The process is also called a banishment and the success rate of the operation is difficult to nail down. How successful this student-led exorcism worked is also a matter of debate.

Right after the ceremony, students claim that far from ridding the room of its paranormal roommate, the activity increased and became more dangerous. Instead of harmless objects moving slightly, sharp objects flew across the room.

On the other hand, there have been fewer and fewer tales of haunting in these dorms over the past decade or so.

Maybe, it just took time for the effects of the banishment to settle in. Or, maybe the spirits just took an off-campus apartment?

UPJ's Haunted Cemetery

There are other spectral suspects said to haunt the grounds of Pitt's Johnstown campus.

The ghost of a small girl has been spotted walking through the campus and drifting in several dorm rooms. In one story, a group of students said they took a walk along the nature trail at UPJ. The students watched as a small girl walked the trail just in front of them.

The girl seemed to recognize the presence of the students, but continued to walk. She disappeared around a turn in the path.

Intrigued, the students assumed the girl, who was too small and too young to be a college student, was visiting her older college-age sibling. But, there was something unsettling about the brief encounter. First, her dress was practically antique, not like anything girls wear today. Another thing caught the group off-guard: she had a "filmy" appearance.

Intrigue transformed to fear. After all, they knew the rumors that the ghost of a girl haunts the campus. She is buried just up the path in the small cemetery that borders the southern edge of the UPJ campus, right behind the paranormally-active athletic fields.

When the students made the turn in the trail, hoping to see a real-live human girl still walking ahead of them, they saw nothing. The girl had vanished.

The students wondered: Did they just see the ghost of the UPJ cemetery?

According to a *Johnstown Tribune-Democrat* story, the University bought a 360-acre piece of land that included the cemetery back in 1966. There's no indication, however, when the ghost of the girl began to show up in UPJ's lengthy haunted lore.

But the theory of the ghost girl is borne out by research done by the area's genealogists and historians. The cemetery is sometimes referred to as Baumgardner Cemetery. The Baumgardner family lived on the plot years before the University purchased the land near the graveyard. Ruins of the old farm can still be seen near the plot of land.

The cemetery contains about 85 graves—many unmarked or barely marked—and is one of the largest private cemeteries in Richland Township. The strangest markers are called Fieldstones. For the plain, hardworking farmers, ornate headstones were rare. The families, instead, marked flat rocks with initials of the deceased and the dates of their death.

It's easy to see why a cemetery so close to campus would inspire a ghost story or two among the students. After all, based on the hundreds of other college ghost stories, placing a cemetery on or near a university campus is going to increase the probability of a few campus legends cropping up. But the details of the ghost stories at this cemetery is different. These details convince paranormal experts that there's something more to the tales than the typical over-active collegiate imagination.

One example: Most of the witnesses say they see a young girl. She's dressed in clothes of an earlier time period, often believed to be late 19th century, or early 20th century garb.

The cemetery would contain graves of people who died during that exact period.

Here's where things get eerie. According to the genealogical study of the cemetery, the remains of several children lie in the quiet cemetery. And, several of these children were girls of the age described by the witnesses. Markers testify to this tragic loss of young lives. One stone is etched in letters now dulled and faded by the encroachment of time lists another of children and infants who died before their full flower of life.

Another stone reads "Children of M & E Baumgardner." The third stone segment reads "Loved In Life," then "In Death Remembered."

These stone markers are perhaps the most substantial manifestation of the sorrow felt for innocent lives that were cut far too short.

But, could there be other manifestations of the emotion and grief that surrounds the death of a child? Could the apparition of the girl seen strolling along the nature trail be a marker of a different sort? Could it be that UPJ students walking along the nature trail have somehow stumbled onto a spiritual echo of the past?

The ghost may yet remind us of one more thing: there is a whole world to explore just outside of the laboratories and classrooms that make up one of Pitt's most haunted branch campuses.

Is It Irony? Living and Learning Center

The previous stories are the best-known and better-documented legends of UPJ. But, there are others.

Wrapped in whispers and rumors, other buildings at UPJ land on the campus's "also haunted" list. The Living/Learning Center, a thoroughly modern residence unit, is one of those places. It seems to be an unlikely spot to catch a sighting of a ghost. The facility was constructed in 1994 and features modern conveniences. That's pretty modern to build a haunted history.

But, according to a few reports that have filtered in, apparitions have been seen in the building. Spectral noises have been heard, as well. **The Complete Idiot's Guide to Ghosts and Hauntings** reports that there are a number of ghosts there, including the ghost of a boy and a woman. More distressing for students who like to sleep in, there are even tales of the ghost of an old man who screams at students when they're asleep. (Wonder if he has a snooze button for those 8 a.m. classes?)

A few other buildings are tagged as haunted at UPJ.

If rumors are to be believed Woodlawn Terrace and Briar Lodge have some haunted activity. Residents have talked and posted messages on the internet about weird noises heard in those buildings, too.

Chapter 10

UPG—Greensburg's Paranormal Campus

The small, but thriving community of Greensburg has a long history that neatly traces the nation's own. The town, situated about 45 minutes south east of Pittsburgh, was named after Revolutionary War hero Nathanael Greene. The community matured during the Industrial Revolution, becoming a vital transportation and mining link for the industrial colossus of Pittsburgh.

Greensburg's place in history is well known. Its place as a center for paranormal history is even more established.

Hidden in the woods of the Allegheny Mountains, the small town of Kecksburg is close Greensburg. The town is world famous in paranormal circles as the site of a reported UFO crash. The story goes that on December 9, 1965, a strange object streaked across the sky above Kecksburg, glanced off the treetops, and crashed into the woods outside of town.

The crash attracted onlookers and, ominously, members of the law enforcement community and the military. Some witnesses, before they were rushed off the crash site by soldiers, said they saw a craft that resembled an acorn smoldering in the middle of the woods.

Military and government officials produced a range of explanations for the night's events. The crash was nothing more than fragments of a meteorite, or a piece of a Russian satellite that re-entered the earth's atmosphere.

The witnesses and other experts on the case who don't buy the military's explanation say that Kecksburg, like Roswell, is part of a massive government cover-up.

Ever since the Kecksburg crash, the Greensburg area was placed on the map for paranormal adventurers who visit Roswell, Area 51, and Gulf Breeze. In fact, Kecksburg has been referred to as "Pennsylvania's Roswell."

But, as the lengthy lore about the University of Pittsburgh at Greensburg (UPG) will demonstrate, UFOs aren't the only paranormal phenomena that you'll encounter in a visit to this corner of Pennsylvania, especially when you tour this jewel in the crown of Pitt's campus system.

UPG is haunted, really haunted, students report. Campus stories pinpoint two buildings in particular as the most haunted buildings on campus—Lynch Hall and Rossetti House.

We'll start with Lynch Hall.

Lynch Hall was a grand, tudor mansion that belonged to Commander Charles McKenna Lynch. The Commander was an executive for the H.C. Frick Coke Company, which had a number of facilities in the Greensburg area.

According to a story in the *Pittsburgh Tribune Review*, Charles graduated from the U.S. Naval Academy. That's the most likely reason why people nicknamed him "Commander." Besides being a war hero, he became a community leader, heading banking and brokerage businesses. He was even the president of the Pittsburgh Stock Exchange.

Constructed in 1923, the Commander's mansion rested on an impressive estate. It was dubbed—nautically—the Starboard Light.

In 1963, the Commander died and the mansion eventually passed into the hands of the University of Pittsburgh. The mansion actually became the centerpiece for the nascent campus, serving as a functional administration building—and a postcard backdrop for the budding campus.

But it wasn't just the architecture that had students and visitors talking about Lynch Hall. It wasn't the aesthetics. It wasn't even the vast interior that gave UPG plenty of room to expand. It was Lynch Hall's ghost—or, depending on whom you talk to, maybe even ghosts.

It seemed like as soon as Pitt officials started to renovate the building, stories began to surface that the mansion had an unexpected resident on the premises.

At first, the tales were brushed off as over-active imaginations. Indeed, in the right light (or the right darkness, to be more precise), Lynch Hall and its sharp angles and pointed towers are text book haunted house material.

But it was more than just the appearance that was a little unsettling. Despite laughing off the first reports of haunted activity, more official reports began to seep in. The stories of ghostly encounters didn't come from a few inebriated college kids, or a couple of visitors caught up in the intimidating size and solemn history of Lynch Hall; these reports came from some of the most respected and most trained observers in the University of Pitt system: University guards.

Security guards who have the unenviable task of watching over Lynch Hall in the depths of night were among of the first campus officials to acknowledge the paranormal presence in the building.

Guards reported that once night fell and darkness invaded the mansion, the building filled with strange sights and sounds. Guards even reported running into a filmy, but unmistakable human presence while making their rounds in the mansion. They swore it was the ghost of Commander Lynch.

The stories of encounters with the Commander's ghost spread. It even reached the heirs of the Commander. When the great-grand children of the Commodore took a tour of Lynch Hall, the family made sure they inquired about the hall's haunted presence. The security guard obliged with a slew of stories that detailed strange run-ins and incidents at Lynch Hall.

Most of the sightings happen in the area of the building that used to be the Commander's office, the officers told the family. This section contains the office, two bedrooms, and a spiral staircase.

In one instance, the guard said that during the nightly rounds she went into the second-floor bathroom to close and lock a window. As she exited, she was shocked to see movement in the room's bathtub. A sad-eyed man sat in the tub, his knees clenched into his body. The man never spoke, but "telepathically" conveyed a question to the frightened guard: "What are you doing in my bathroom?"

The guard, not believing her own eyes, quickly looked away and then looked again, hoping that when she turned her head again the apparition would have turned out to be a figment of her imagination.

No such luck.

He was still there.

She ran to get another guard. When they came back, the man was gone, but the guards were speechless when they saw that the window was open again and the bathroom door appeared to also be cracked open.

The ghost was not quite finished with this intrepid guard. She said in another instance, she walked to the main door of Lynch Hall and saw a figure at the top of the stairs. He was leaning on the railing and was dressed in the clothes of an earlier period.

He said, "Well, are you coming in" to the guard.

She didn't accept the invitation. Although she said she didn't feel threatened, she refused to go in.

The Commander didn't just appear to people in uniform. One workman reported to the guards that he saw a man in a blue dress uniform. It was an apt description of the type of uniform a U.S. Naval officer or a graduate of the U.S. Naval Academy would have worn. The guards were not surprised. They knew exactly who the sailor was.

Finally, a psychic had been called in to offer her impressions of the building. As soon as she entered the hall, she was floored by the supernatural vibrations. She reported to others that she felt the presence of a male spirit. Without any apparent prior knowledge of the building's haunted history, the psychic correctly repeated details of the encounter with the ghost in the bathroom. The psychic reassured the guards that the ghost was not evil; he was actually being playful.

The members of the Lynch family and others who knew the Commander are split about who the source of the haunting is. One side of the family says this doesn't sound like the Commander, who was not much of a prankster. They also believe the former naval officer would identify himself.

However, others in the family say the apparition seen in Lynch Hall is without question Commander Lynch. During tours, one great-grandchild of the Commander felt—and perhaps saw—a presence in the section that is reportedly the hub of this haunting. The descendant detailed the encounter on a message board:

"I could feel something in one of the bedrooms and it made me catch my breath and my eyes water, I could feel something or someone was there. I was face to face with him, but could not see him. Although, I did see some motion in the air. It had kind of a fluid look, and I'm sure it wasn't my eyes.

"I simply said, 'Why are you here Great Grandfather, you need to go on?' Then I left the room to catch my breath. I know someone or something is in that house. I would like to help him make his peace with God."

Another question people ask is: Why is Lynch Hall haunted?

The Commander lived a contented life, it seems. Not to say that hauntings are always caused by sad moments, but tales of misfortune often linger behind haunted legends. Oddly, tragedy doesn't seem to be especially affixed to Lynch Hall as it is in other reputed haunted homes. No suicides or murders or accidental deaths appear to have occurred at Lynch Hall.

There is one interesting speculation.

They say the activity is caused by renovations to the mansion. Renovation work is actually a frequently-cited reason for homes that were once supernaturally quiet to suddenly burst into paranormal activity.

The renovations to Lynch Hall—which even the living seem to complain about—may have stirred the Commander's activity. Maybe he is upset that his sanctuary has been disturbed.

Or he just doesn't like the new decor.

And that's all you need: the ghost of a naval officer who thinks he's an interior decorator.

Spirit Communications 101: G-E-T- O-U-T

In 2008 a group of brave UPG students decided to take the spirit matters of Lynch Hall into their own hands. Led by two resident advisers and armed with candles and a Ouija board, about 35 students struck off to the basement of the infamous hall to see if they could communicate with the phantom full-time naval officer, part-time interior decoration critic.

The article, which appeared in the *Pittsburgh Tribune-Review*, detailed the adventure. Before the investigation, the RA's made sure to prime the student spirit-seekers with a brief talk about Charles McKenna Lynch and offered a full disclosure of the ghost sightings in the building, especially the story about the campus police officer who refuses to work the night shift at Lynch Hall. After a brief glimpse of Lynch's portrait (so the students could identify the ghost), the group was ready for the séance.

With the Ouija board set on the floor and two candles flickering in the dark, the students began to ask the spirits—if there were any in the premises—questions. As the pointer, called a planchette, drifted along the board and appeared to be guided toward a jumble of letters on the board, some more definite answers came through.

When the students asked if Lynch was present, the word "YES" was spelled out.

Things were about to get creepier.

As the séance continued, the sound of water began to echo in the basement. While students assumed a guard had flushed the toilet in one of the floors above them, the sound continued... and continued.

As far as they knew, no one else was in the building.

The students asked the Ouija board if the Commander was responsible for the sounds. Again, the board replied: "Yes."

The next message was even more disturbing for some of the students. When they asked whether the spirit wanted them to leave, the reply, "G-E-T O-U-T," was methodically spelled out.

About half the group accepted the spirit's invitation and bolted for the Lynch Hall door.

Natalie Czmola, one of the students who attended the outing told the reporter, "The fact it said, 'Get out,' I'm not comfortable with that. It creeps me out, but it's interesting."

Not everyone ducked out at the first indication of supernatural conflict. A group of students continued to ask questions and the spirit grew more agitated.

When the students asked if the spirit had something to tell the world, the word "HELLP" was spelled out. The pointer slid across the board to the "yes" mark when the group asked if the spirit was trapped on earth and then spelled out "DEATH."

The spirit had one more message for the students who asked if the spirit planned to visit any other campus buildings that night. "RS" was the reply.

Did the spirit just spell out the initials of the Robertshaw dorm—the home of most of these spirit-seeking students?

Whether the spirit really did move the planchette to communicate with the students, or the subconscious desires of the Ouija Board operators directed the answers, it's a good bet that students who attended the Lynch Hall séance that night slept a little less soundly at Robertshaw.

What's a Ouija Board?

A Ouija board, or spirit board, is a flat board with letters and numbers printed on it. Participants put their finger tips on the planchette, a movable piece that serves as a pointer. The participants ask questions and the spirit, supposedly, uses the planchette to pick letters that spell out the response.

The Ouija, which is a combination of the French (Oui) and German (ja) words for yes, is a controversial tool of ghost hunters and paranormal researchers. Some say that if you use the board, spirits use you as intermediaries. If the spirit is evil, he—or she—

may not want to leave. So use Ouija with caution!

The Rossetti House

Lynch Hall has the best pedigree for BHOC: the Big Haunt on Campus. It has all the typical traits of the quintessential haunted house: old mansion, spacious interior, larger-than-life former owner, and an extensive renovation effort.

But there's another place on campus that students and even some professors and staff members say is UPG's second biggest supernatural hot spot. It's called the Rossetti House.

From the outside, the Rossetti House doesn't appear to be that haunted, not when you compare it to Lynch Hall. It was once a charming 1940 Sears Roebuck house that was converted into a University building.

The Rossetti House, too, is connected to the Lynch family and, as we discovered in our tour of Lynch Hall, they are a prodigiously paranormal family. The Rossetti House was built originally for Mary Quinn, daughter of Charles McKenna Lynch—the Commander who supposedly makes his paranormal presence known in Lynch Hall.

The Rossetti House, which was renamed after the late Dr. Guy Rossetti, a former Pitt-Greensburg official, is now used as an admissions building for the campus. The busy workers in the building must have inadvertently approved a few admission applications for ghosts and poltergeists because, over the years, paranormal reports have piled up in the building like stacks of student admission essays.

Visitors say that the building is filled with strange knocks and noises that erupt unexpectedly and without a human source. It's not just the casual visitor who notices, either. Veteran staff members are all-too familiar with the noises that echo in the Rossetti House.

One long-time, respected staff member, Janet "Dolly" Biskup, mentioned both the

Lynch Hall and Rossetti House ghost tales of UPG when she told a campus publication, "I know one staff member who swears she saw the ghost of Commander Lynch, and I've heard students talk about strange noises in Rossetti House, which originally was the home of Mrs. Quinn."

But who—or what—is the source of the haunting?

Most people assume the bumps in the night (and during the day, too) are the work of Mary Quinn. The paranormal buffs have a list of reasons why she's causing the disturbance. She may be trying to keep up with her spirit-manifesting father, or she just might be mad that the school dubbed her home, the Rossetti House, not the Quinn House.

Whatever the reason, using a haunted house as an admissions office for UPG is a great way to offer new students a paranormal welcome to one of the most haunted campuses in the University of Pittsburgh system.

Chapter 11

Titusville Area Terrors

Like its companion campus at Bradford, the town of Titusville grew out of the Pennsylvania oil boom.

Its history—and its haunted history—starts way before that oil strike, though. The history of Titusville goes back to 1796 when Jonathan Titus settled the wild area. Others soon joined the experiment and Titus named the small village Edinburg.

Driven by the lumber industry, the town was already a bustling community when prospectors hit oil. Then, it became an absolute boom town.

Soon after, it became a boom town of a different sort—a supernatural one.

Almost as soon as the oil money paved the way for the construction of opulent mansions and magnificent public buildings and theaters in the region, the stories of ghosts began to creep out of the night.

The oil boom died out. But the ghost stories never did.

It was in this spooky environment that the administrators of the University of Pittsburgh established a campus. The campus was established in 1963 to serve the needs of the Oil Creek Region.

UPT's first classes were held in McKinney Hall.

McKinney Hall was once a mansion on the McKinney estate and campus rests on land that once made up part of the McKinney estate. The mansion, a sprawling Victorian, was built in 1870 and was donated to the University of Pittsburgh in 1963 for the purpose of opening a college in the region.

So, we have an old, sprawling mansion that was converted into a college building. Sounds like a perfect place for a few campus legends, or a University of Pitt ghost, right?

Apparently not.

Despite reams of research, there doesn't seem to be a ghost in McKinney Hall. It's a quiet place paranormally speaking. At least no one has documented it.

What about the nearby Carriage House? It certainly has the necessary transcripts to apply for a Titusville haunted house.

Not so much.

In fact, it's hard to find any verified case of haunting on the campus of UPT.

What gives?

Could it be that since UPT is a relatively new campus and that no ghosts have had a chance to settle in to the collegiate lifestyle?

Or, could it be that all the spirits went to the super-haunted Johnstown and Greensburg campuses?

There's another theory.

Ghosts don't need to haunt a short strip of campus land in Titusville—no matter how nice and scholarly the surroundings are—when they have a whole town to themselves. The attractively named, Pithole City, lies just beyond the confines of the UPT campus.

It's a remnant of what followed Pennsylvania's oil boom—the oil bust.

The oil bust created ghost towns almost overnight. Pithole City was one of those ghost towns. The town was actually just a piece of a farm when oil was discovered just beneath the farm's soil.

According to **Pennsylvania Ghost Towns**, the origin of the town's odd name was either nefarious, or sulfurous. Some just say Pithole refers to the holes left by prospectors looking for oil wells. Other say the area was a portal to hell.

Sulfurous gases emanating from the rocks were evidence enough to conclude there was something diabolical afoot in the region.

For those who consider stories of Pithole City's evil spirits as mere myth and urban legends, true believers point to the town's strange rise—and sudden fall—as additional proof.

Legend has it that two speculators—one named Frazier and the other, Faulkner—discovered oil on the property by using occult powers. Taking a branch of witch hazel, the two "doused" to locate their oil well. In January 1865 the well was constructed and soon was pumping out 350 barrels a day, a huge amount at the time.

The site became a mecca of fortune seekers—and plenty of lost souls.

In 1865, 15,000 residents called Pithole City home. There were 57 hotels. And a couple brothels.

The town even had its own newspaper.

Structures went up overnight. Literally. The two-story Astor Hotel was built in a day.

While the buildings flourished, no one thought about the infrastructure. Conditions were truly hellish with no garbage removal and no sanitary facilities. People took off their shoes and socks to cross the street. When they got to the other side, they washed their feet off in buckets.

Those buckets of water must've cost a pretty penny back then, too. With no water wells in the town, a cup of water cost a dime.

The town was described as smelling like, "a camp full of soldiers with diarrhea."

Cleanliness and crowded conditions quickly led to disease. And death.

But typhus, dysentery, and other nasty bugs weren't the only concerns facing the good citizens of Pithole City. A cast of unsavory crooks and criminals were drawn to the town's easy money and laissez faire approach to law enforcement.

Boxer Ben Hogan and his prostitute girlfriend, French Kate, were residents of Pithole.

Hogan billed himself as "the wickedest man in the world" and soon tried to live up to that reputation. He had some competition. John Wilkes Booth, Abraham Lincoln's assassin, was once a citizen of Pithole City.

He was suspected in range of nefarious activities including kidnapping and starting riots. French Kate certainly tried to match her boyfriend's evil legacy. She was the town's main madame who had her "employees" advertise their services by riding horses naked through the town.

If crime and disease weren't enough to kick up the paranormal powers in Pithole City, the numerous accidents surely produced a gusher of ghosts. During one infamous accident, a group of Pithole City citizens gathered around a well that was going to hit oil.

As the curiosity-seekers waited, the well horrifically exploded. Accounts report nearly twenty people were injured. One person later died in a hospital.

More fires and destruction followed. Without access to water, a small fire could consume several structures.

Just a few years later, Pithole City was no more. In 1877, the town's borough charter was annulled. In 1879, the million-dollar town was sold to Venango County for a couple of bucks.

Now, nothing is left besides a small visitor's center, remnants of buildings—and ghosts.

Pithole City is now a target for the Oil region's ghost hunters and paranormal researchers.

Mixing high tech and ancient tech, the investigators try to collect evidence that the ghost town isn't deserted quite yet. They use precise digital thermometers to detect any sudden shifts in temperatures. Ghosts, they say, draw energy when they manifest. When they do, the temperature can drop as this energy is pulled from the environment.

The teams also carry recording devices hoping to capture electronic voice phenomena, or EVPs. Pithole City investigators say you can use this equipment to pick up voices of Pithole City's former citizens. Their voices are heard at low volume levels or masked by static.

Paranormal researchers say that Pithole City is an obvious place to test their ghost-catching technology. According to one theory on the supernatural, areas of intense emotions can cause ripples or indentations in the time-space fabric. These indentations are like grooves of a record player—or, if you're too young to remember primitive record players, bits of data on a mp3. These spiritual grooves keep playing in the form of sound phenomena and even apparitions.

It's often referred to as "residual phenomena" by paranormal researchers.

Groups who have investigated Pithole City say that they have come back with recordings of strange voices.

Are these the voices of the lost spirits of Pithole City? Or are they just electromagnetic interference that, like the way shapes of objects, animals, and people are found in clouds, become words and phrases to the ears of believers.

It's just, perhaps, one more mystery left at Pithole City, Pennsylvania's most famous ghost town.

Paranormal Pitt Afterword

Why is Pitt Haunted?

We've established one thing: the University of Pittsburgh is home to a lot of great ghost stories.

In fact, Pitt isn't unusual in this regard; most universities have their share of ghost stories and spooky lore.

But it does seem that if a Dean's List existed for paranormal activity, Pitt would be at the top.

So, why is Pitt so haunted?

There are primarily three reasons why Pitt is the place for haunted legends.

The first is geographic. Pitt just happens to be situated in a region where ghost stories and legends have a lot of credence.

We've established that folklore is a vibrant tradition in the Pittsburgh area. When cultures and tragedies collide, legends are established. While this is true across the country and around the world, the Steel City is especially prone to legend-making. Battles and industrial calamities, natural disasters and man-made tragedies have created the perfect conditions for ghost stories.

Secondly, culturally-speaking, Pittsburgh is a melting pot. Immigrants from all over the world were drawn to the area for jobs and a new life. The rise of Andrew Carnegie from immigrant to industrialist is one Pittsburgh success story. When cultures come together, they often seek a common story. Ghost stories and legends fit that common bond.

The final reason for hauntings at the University of Pittsburgh and its branch campuses relates to the above theory. If Pittsburgh is a culturally dynamic city—with new groups of people moving in all the time—then Pitt's even more dynamic. A university has what you would call a "transitory population." Each year a whole new group of students move in, while another group moves out.

Ghost stories and legends are "sticky." They become a way of conveying history easily and memorably. You only have to hear tales about the hauntings in the Cathedral of Learning once to get a good sense of the building's place in the city and University's history, as well as understand the background of the cast of characters that makes Pitt such a vibrant place to learn and to conduct research.

Sometimes, in a single story, you can learn more about the University than a dozen tour guides can provide. And, these stories tend to be viral. With each incoming class, tales of cafeteria poltergeists and strange ghosts of Alumni Hall are spread quickly and efficiently.

These legends also convey the school's customs and attitudes. The legend of the sleeping ballerina, for instance, can teach students about paying attention—or at least getting a good night's sleep.

Of course, these stories of ghosts and spirits may not be fictional pieces of folklore. We can't discount the possibility that some of these stories are based on fact. Paranormal researchers suggest that the trauma of these misfortunes may have embedded into the very fabric of reality and are now transformed into the paranormal phenomena. The final theory for the supernatural at Pitt probably keeps more students up at night than an early morning Statistics final. Could it be that there are paranormal forces at work in the University and at its branch campuses?

Could there actually be spirits of industrialists walking the halls at night? Could the vibrant personalities of some of Pittsburgh's most famous women be so powerful that even death could not stop them?

Could ghost towns be actually full of ghosts?

Before you answer the questions, take a solo tour of the Cathedral of Learning some autumn night. And then let me know what you think.

Tip: How to Protect Your Place from Paranormal Activity

Believers in the supernatural are generally separated into two camps: those who embrace the paranormal, and those who fear it.

The embracers welcome an encounter with a ghost. They'll even encourage the interaction by holding seances and using a Ouija board to contact the dead. You'll find these folks creeping around dark halls with tape recorders hoping to catch electronic voice phenomena (EVPs), or wielding video cameras to capture video evidence of a ghostly encounter.

At the other extreme, there are people who are terrified of encountering the unknown. Students, who are already stressed enough with exams and term papers, are among those who don't need another reason to stay up late.

For those students, paranormal researchers and occult specialists offer a few ways to minimize haunted activity.

Burn Sage Incense

Sage was used by Native Americans to purify an area. Burning a little sage (often called a smudge stick) can help cleanse a space from evil spirits, occult experts say. Buying a sage-based incense stick should do the trick, as well.

Pray

Prayers of protection can also be recited in each room. Those worried about a non-living presence can rely on whatever prayer is considered a blessing in their religious backgrounds.

Deal with negative psychological issues

As weird as it sounds, it's often a person who is haunted—not his or her space. Poltergeist outbreaks, for example, are often tied to a human who is suffering from psychological trauma. The person, called an agent, uses telekinesis to create this paranormal activity. Since college students are often stressed out by the academic and social strains of university life, experts say this can build into uncontrolled telekinetic outbursts. Working out those issues can help resolve the poltergeist phenomena.

Blessings

A quick blessing can assuage some spirits, experts say. To conduct a blessing, walk through the rooms of your dorm, apartment, or home and recite a prayer of blessing from your religion or faith tradition out loud. You may want to have a friend or friends accompany you—the combined spiritual power can increase the effectiveness of your blessing.

Avoid Confrontations

Many victims of paranormal hazings feel frustrated and want to fight back. That can be a mistake. Experts say confrontation, if not done by a trained handler, can lead to an escalation in the phenomena.

Say No to Ouija

Even the most casual viewer of horror movies knows the following: never use a Ouija Board to contact spirits.

Those familiar with the occult say it's not bad advice.

To use the Ouija Board, people lightly place their hands on a planchette. In theory, the spirit channeled through the users pushes the planchette along the board to land on a letter, number, or a yes-no space to answer questions from the group.

Unfortunately, the spirit may not be the nicest ghost on the block. This combined fearful psychic energy generated by the group can give the spirit more power, not less.

Another warning experts give: since the spirit world can transcend time and space, the spirit picked up on the Ouija Board might not be your nice, friendly home ghost; it might be a nefarious entity looking for an open channel.

Resources:

Spooky Pennsylvania by S.E. Schossler, Globe Pequot.

The Complete Idiots Guide to Ghosts, Tom Ogden, Alpha

The Original Magazine

Johnstown Tribune Democrat

Pittsburgh Post Gazette

Pennsylvania Ghost Towns, Uncovering the hidden past, Susan Hutchison Tassin, Stackpole Books

http://www.post-gazette.com/pg/09304/1009748-298.stm

http://hauntsandhistory.blogspot.com/2008/08/byers-lyons-mansion.htmlarlow
http://www.camgenpa.com/cems/RicBaumgardner01.html

Note: Investigating the paranormal can be fun and rewarding. However, make sure you have permission from the correct authorities and property owners before you investigate a property that's reportedly haunted. Failure to do so can lead to arrest and lawsuits.

Made in the USA
Middletown, DE
13 July 2017